In order to strengthen the bond
with the Netherlands and in particular
with Ermelo I present you
this beautiful book of Dutch impressions

Also on behalf of the people of Ermelo
I wish you all the best and above all
a lot of pleasure with the concerts
of the Ermelo male choir

Wiert P. Omta

postadres: Postbus 500, 3850 AM Ermelo
bezoekadres: Raadhuisplein 2
tel. (0341) 56 73 21 telefax (0341) 56 73 69

HOLLAND
in motion

Ouddorp / Zuid-Holland

Martin Kers

HOLLAND
in motion

Text: Marijke Kers

TERRA

Johannes Kerkhovenpolder / Groningen

Foreword

The calibre of Martin Kers' work as landscape photographer over the years emerges not only from the quality of his photographs but also from the eagerness with which clients, like National Geographic and Holland Herald, have seized the opportunity to publish what his eyes have seen and his hand and mind have recorded. There was good reason to assume, therefore, that a second 'Holland book' would be forthcoming fairly soon.

Clearly Martin Kers' vision has not changed. But his photographs have, or rather Holland has. The country has become fuller, industrial activity has increased and agriculture and lifestock farming have imposed, and partially realised, their claims on space and the environment.

It is almost a cliché to point out how all the factors can jeopardise our physical planning and our environment. But that is the reality, and all of us need to realise that it depends on us whether we can keep things under control and ensure that our country is healthy. Photographs can help us.

The fourth Physical Planning Report Extra (VINEX) sets forth the possibilities and impossibilities for urbanisation into the next century. The size of the so-called Green Heart in the Randstad conurbation, and the encroachments upon it, are being debated virtually daily. And that can do no harm. Talking with each other means we have a fair chance of agreeing with each other. Photographs can help us here too.

I do not intend to dwell on the threats to our environment here. Martin Kers has presented us with a record of our country as it now stands. Including the threats, but also including what has been preserved, and what must be preserved. In this he has succeeded excellently.

Margaretha de Boer
Minister of Housing, Spatial Planning and the Environment

Camperduin / Noord-Holland

Long before our era began giant breakers and strong
winds threw high sand walls on our coast.
Storms took their turns to draw many a dune back
into the sea. In the interval all seems quiet and
peaceful. Even today dunes come and go during
heavy storms.

Camperduin / Noord-Holland

ABOVE: *Schipborg / Drenthe*

BELOW: *Waddinxveen / Zuid-Holland*

ABOVE: *Uithoorn / Noord-Holland*

BELOW: *Kantens / Groningen*

Nothing is more pleasant than a bicycle trip through the
countryside or to a particular destination. Nothing is
more frustrating though, than to lose your way because
there are no signposts, or worse still, because they are
pointing the wrong way. Add to this a flat tire,
with no repair kit on hand to help you.

ABOVE: *Johannes Kerkhovenpolder / Groningen*   BELOW: *Eilandspolder / Noord-Holland*

ABOVE: *Oudemirdum / Friesland*

BELOW: *Nisse / Zeeland*

Look deeply into a cow's large dewy eyes, as it gazes
serenely at its surroundings. The pink nose exhaling
a white haze, sniffing at times. Its big mouth is
silent. Sometimes a low mooing breaks the stillness
of the meadow. From time to time its tongue
moistens its lips, then all is quiet.
The cow exists in its own hazy silence.

ABOVE: *Grootschermer / Noord-Holland*   BELOW: *Dordrecht / Kop van het Land / Zuid-Holland*

In the Netherlands vast areas of water have been transformed into polders. New land where previously
no-one could live. Water boards supervise these areas.
They are mainly responsible for the water level,
the maintenance of the dikes, and the cleaning and
pollution control of the waterways and ditches.

ABOVE: *Waal / Opijnen / Gelderland*

BELOW: *Waal / Oosterhout / Gelderland*

Germany is an important trading partner. Thousands of privately owned barges transport goods back and forth over the major rivers, the Rhine and the Waal, between Germany and the transit harbour of Rotterdam. River signposts, rules and regulations control the traffic on the rivers and small piers protect the banks from erosion.

Kampen / Overijssel

From Arnhem the IJssel meanders slowly to the
Ketelmeer. Here and there a small ferry crosses
the river. Near the larger towns such as Zutphen,
Deventer, Zwolle and Kampen bridges link the two
banks.

Meerkerk / Zuid-Holland

A pedestrian bridge, also used by cyclists, crosses the
Merwedekanaal. This canal connects the Waal with the
Lek at Vianen.

ABOVE: *Smallebrugge / Jeltesloot / Friesland*   BELOW: *Maasbruggen / Rotterdam / Zuid-Holland*

ABOVE: *Afsluitdijk / Kornwerderzand / Friesland*

BELOW: *Tollebeek / Flevoland*

Bridges, whether they are moveable or fixed, form the most important link between areas separated by water. Their construction is the culmination of technical data, formulas and figures. Their size and shape depend to a large extent on the number of people using them and how they wish to cross them.

Vijfheerenlanden / Zuid-Holland

Five families dominated the history of this region.
Each family has given its name to a town or village i.e.
Arkel, Vianen, Everdingen, Hagestein and Leerdam.
With the exception of the A 37 motorway which cuts
through this area, Vijfheerenlanden has remained
relatively unspoilt to this day.

Reeuwijk-Brug / Zuid-Holland

More advanced techniques have made it possible to
drain the Zuid-Holland lakes to an even lower level.
Old peat bogs have been transformed into extensive
grasslands. Fortunately some have survived the urge for
reclamation and still exist in their natural state.

Vuilendam / Zuid-Holland

The banks of small waterways are connected by low lying
bridges, either fixed or moveable. The latter can be either
draw- or swing bridges which enable boats to pass through.
These clever constructions are worthy of a separate study.

ABOVE: *Brouwersdam / Zuid-Holland*   BELOW: *Greffeling / Gelderland*

A traditional pastime is daydreaming at the edge of
a lake, lazily watching birds, water lilies or the reeds
swaying in the breeze. The shimmering water surface
forms the border between the visible above and the
invisible below. The temptation to muse, to idle or
to handle a fishing rod simply cannot be resisted.

ABOVE: *Maurik / Gelderland*

Water is important in all seasons. In the summer
there is swimming and boating.
Then as November nears everyone hopes
that frost will turn the water into ice.

BELOW: *Schillaard / Friesland*

What can be a more beautiful sight than the skaters
touring or waltzing, and the speed skaters competing
with each other! To be able to stand and walk
on the ice and look at the surroundings from
a different angle.

ABOVE: *Lelystad / Flevoland*

The water level in the Netherlands is measured according to NAP, the Amsterdam reference level (ARL), the mean level of the North Sea. The ARL is universally recognised, just like weights and measures are.

BELOW: *Oosterzee / Friesland*

The ARL lies invisible under the Dam in Amsterdam, but it was placed where it could be seen when the new town hall was built. However, as this was not very practical, thousands of reference levels have been placed throughout the country.

ABOVE: *Bovenkerk / Noord-Holland*   BELOW: *Beneden-Leeuwen / Gelderland*

Eenigenburg / Noord-Holland

The very old West Frisian ring dike curves for more than
120 kilometres along the IJsselmeer and Westfriesland via
Schagen towards Alkmaar, passing Schermerhorn on its way
to Hoorn. Beyond the dike are the much lower Zijpe- and
Hazepolders and the Schermer and the Beemster.
These reclaimed polders each have their unique traits.

Eenigenburg / Noord-Holland

Driebruggen / Zuid-Holland

The reservoirs, the Enkele Wiericke and Dubbele Wiericke, just west of Driebruggen, flow into the Oude Rijn. These waterways form part of the Dutch Water Defense "the Waterlinie". The Dutch already recognised the value of water as a defense weapon during the 80 years war against the Spanish.

Driebruggen / Zuid-Holland

Mud from ditch maintenance was for a long time used
as fertilizer. It is hardly used as such any more.
To keep the water at a safe level, farmers are required by
law to clear the ditches on their land, in order not to
prevent regular drainage.

ABOVE: *Grosthuizen / Noord-Holland*   BELOW: *Termunterzijl / Groningen*

ABOVE: *Montfoort / Utrecht*

BELOW: *Zuid-Beijerland / Zuid-Holland*

A fence is a symbol for ownership. It also serves to keep the cattle enclosed. Visually of course, there is no barrier. Fences have appeared all through history in all cultures. A fence serves a purpose. If it is damaged or lacking the consequences may create problems. Sheep could stray and pigs may wander into the wheat fields.

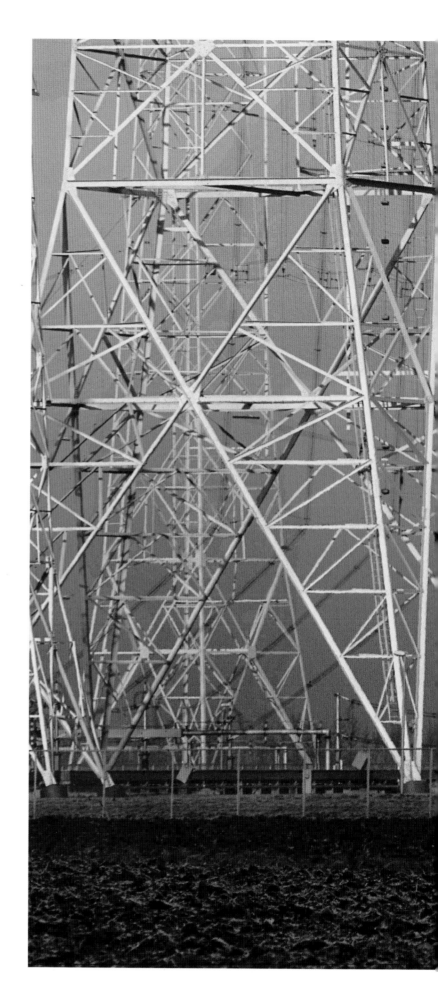

Flevopolder / Flevoland

Nature reserves, recreational areas and towns had already been planned in detail before the Zuiderzee was reclaimed in 1953. However, increasing the agricultural area was the primary objective of the act of 1918 which set in motion this vast undertaking, changing the map of the Netherlands.

Vijfheerenlanden / Zuid-Holland

The much higher situated river Lek fringes the
northernmost point of Vijfheerenlanden.
An ingenious system of 13 windmills prevented,
right up to the 19th century, the area from flooding.
After the construction of the Merwedekanaal the
superfluous water was pumped into the canal.

Nieuwe Wetering / Zuid-Holland

The combination of water and extensive farmlands attracts large numbers of birds. Their breeding and foraging grounds are being encroached upon due to increasing urbanisation. Only the Blue Heron is not deterred. Even in busy city centres it is able to cope.

ABOVE: *Dreumel / Gelderland*

Between the banks of the Waal and the dike lie the water meadows. Narrow paths wind their way across them. Low fences and trees mark the landscape. When the water is at a low level, especially in the summer, it is an extensive grazing ground for cattle.

BELOW: *Uiterwaarden / Waal / Gelderland*

Later, in autumn and winter, the water rises, the paths disappear and only the tops of the trees are visible. The cattle are safe in their barns.

ABOVE: *Ophemert / Gelderland*

BELOW: *Giessenburg / Zuid-Holland*

In the open flat lands wind can play havoc with
crops and cattle. Willows and poplars, planted in
neat rows, reduce the force of the wind and act
as a natural barrier.

ABOVE: *Hondsbosse Zeewering / Noord-Holland*

BELOW: *Afsluitdijk / Noord-Holland*

To a large extent the flaxen dunes along our sea
front prevent the sea from flooding our low lands.
However man-made dikes have a greater share in the
defence against the sea. Along the Dutch coast,
including the Wadden islands, hundreds of kilometres of dikes offer protection.

ABOVE: *Oudemirdum / Friesland*

BELOW: *Hondsbosse Zeewering*

Dikes as a sea defence form an important part of
Dutch hydraulic engineering. Governments and
companies all over the world consult our specialists.
Our expertise has become an important
export product.

Delfzijl / Groningen

In the extreme northeast of Groningen, situated
strategically on the Eems river estuary and outside
the sphere of influence of the Randstad in the west,
is the Netherlands sixth harbour, bustling with
activity. Its immediate surroundings, in contrast,
are tranquil and remote.

IJmuiden/Noord-Holland

Even the busiest centres have peaceful havens nearby.
One glance to the right would show the chimneys of the
Hoogovens steelworks blowing their silvery grey
smoke into the sky. Further inland, the town is
steadily growing.

ABOVE: *Ter Heijde / Westland / Zuid-Holland*   BELOW: *Honselersdijk / Westland / Zuid-Holland*

ABOVE: *'s-Gravezande / Westland / Zuid-Holland*

BELOW: *Ter Heijde / Westland / Zuid-Holland*

The horticultural centre of Holland can be justly referred to as a glass city. On maps of the region the greenhouses take up more space than the urban areas. The road system between them is extensive and complicated. Under these glass roofs the largest market garden of Europe is in full swing.

ABOVE: *Weurt / Nijmegen / Gelderland*

BELOW: *Dak van de Bloemenveiling / Honselersdijk / Zuid-Holland*

ABOVE: *Zwolle / Overijssel*

BELOW: *Assen / Drenthe*

Production, construction, innovation and motiva-
tion have introduced their own new language.
Outsiders often do not know the specific terms used,
let alone understand them.

Urk / Noordoostpolder

The capacity to live, move, work, develop and act depends on energy. Energy allows men, animals, plants, instruments and machines to work. Sun, wind and water, coal, oil, gas and atomic energy are sources which cannot be used as such. They first must be converted into electricity.

ABOVE: *Abcoude / Utrecht*

The modern wind turbine converts wind directly
into electricity. The wind energy of the old mills was
directly connected to the machines within the mill.

BELOW: *Dieden / Gelderland*

The force of the wind had its effect on the pace with
which the work in the mill was carried out. Peeling
barley, making mustard, grinding grain, sawing
wood, preparing paper were just a few of the many
activities of the mill.

ABOVE: *Schermerhorn / Noord-Holland*

BELOW: *Kinderdijk / Zuid-Holland*

History recounts the story of the land reclamation.
Vast areas of water which were drained and kept dry
by countless windmills. At the end of the twenties
the electric pumping station replaced the windmills.
However the windmills are capable of taking over
should there be a power failure.

ABOVE: *Bovenkerk / Noord-Holland*

BELOW: *Oude Bildtdijk / Friesland*

Apartment buildings rose out of the ground at great speed to help solve the housing shortage after the second world war.

Cultural changes concerning personal hygiene and individual leisure time as well as changes in the composition of the population and the ever increasing numbers of elderly people have created a new housing problem.

ABOVE: *Dinteloord / Noord-Brabant*

BELOW: *Deventer / Overijssel*

In spite of the housing problem, houses and even apartment buildings are continually being demolished. Demolition and rebuilding is often cheaper than renovation. Sometimes a house has to make way for a new development plan; at other times a creative solution is sought and building simply takes place around the existing house.

ABOVE: *Meerkerk / Zuid-Holland*   BELOW: *Overslingeland / Zuid-Holland*

Environment, reallotment and restructuring are becoming priority items. Due to ever new notions, concepts, rules and regulations each era imposes its mark on the landscape.

ABOVE: *Vaals / Limburg*

BELOW: *Oude Bildtdijk / Friesland*

Continuous changes in the composition of the
population has its effect on the use of land.
The landscape changes perpetually, sometimes
swiftly, sometimes almost unnoticed.

ABOVE: *Zevenhuizen / Zuid-Holland*

The old peat moors of the "green heart" of Holland provide the ideal soil for the cultivation of trees and ornamental plants.

BELOW: *Delden / Overijssel*

Modern farmers must produce more economically to survive. Hence more than 250,000 acres of wheat fields have been replaced by monotonous fields of maize, used for cattle fodder.

ABOVE: *Lelystad / Flevoland*

Step-by-step over a number of years the new polder has been reclaimed and developed. It is a never-ending process. In the summer the once sombre muddy fields are covered by a golden wealth of colza.

BELOW: *Flevopolder / Flevoland*

Fruit trees require special soil. Their roots must grow unhindered for at least one meter in depth. Rainwater should be able to drain away as quickly as possible to prevent the roots from rotting.

Buurserzand / Overijssel

A curtain of trees blocks a clear view of the skyline.
The distance beckons, tempting but aloof.

Eemland / Utrecht

Buttercups, dandelions, daisies, cornflowers, poppies and nettles can all be
defined as weeds, plants which can grow abundantly no matter where.
Nothing is less true. A little too much manure, a less chalky or soured
soil, and they will not appear at all. Insecticides have wiped out
many wild flower species.

ABOVE: *Purmerend / Noord-Holland*   BELOW: *Tricht / Gelderland*

ABOVE: *Wijk bij Duurstede / Utrecht*

BELOW: *Lage Zwaluwe / Noord-Brabant*

A growing number of people require adequate housing. Stricter municipal building requirements now apply for the construction of new houses and the renovation of old ones. Costs, subsidies, building materials and the environment also have to be taken into account.

Oud-Valkenburg / Kasteel Schaloen / Limburg

A mansion with one or more towers is not always a castle. A castle in the proper sense, not only served as living quarters, but also for protection. Nowadays the buildings we refer to as castles have an exclusively residential purpose.

ABOVE: *Het Bildt / Friesland*   BELOW: *Sneek / Friesland*

ABOVE: *Marken / Noord-Holland*

BELOW: *Vondelpark / Amsterdam / Noord-Holland*

Once a year the village celebrates, the town is in a
festive mood, the flags are flying, something unusual
is occurring at the water side. It is the Queen's
birthday. There is feasting, music, brass bands play.
There are street parties, competitions take place.
Villagers cheer. Everyone rises to the occasion.

ABOVE: *Lievelde / Gelderland* BELOW: *Bommelskous / Zuid-Holland*

ABOVE: *Katwijk / Zuid-Holland*

BELOW: *Pingjum / Friesland*

One hundred years ago the British Railway Board, to further their own interests, convinced the government that traffic would be safer if cars were preceded by a man waving a warning flag. In the Netherlands traffic legislation did not appear until 1950 when the official traffic act was passed.

ABOVE: *Spijk / Zuid-Holland*

Only routine cyclists are familiar with the obstacles on their route which are enough to spoil a pleasant journey. Road works for instance, or a bicycle path coming to an abrupt end.

BELOW: *IJzendijke / Zeeland*

Many a cycle trip leads to the other side of a river. It is water which mostly impedes the cyclist's way. Long detours must be taken around lakes and large ponds. Trying to cross a river is no simple matter.

ABOVE: *Peppelenburg / Ede / Gelderland*

Ferries are often at great distances from each other and many bridges do not have cycle paths. This all changed in the early eighties. The ANWB (automobile association) came up with a plan to improve the situation on river bridges.

BELOW: *Dreumel / Gelderland*

The Ministry of Transport and the Railway Board, owners of most bridges, are now providing better facilities for cyclists.

De Heen / Noord-Brabant

Cultural conceptions and religious convictions decide the rites and
services at funerals and cremations. When the convictions change the
proceedings change. Cremations were cautiously introduced into the
Netherlands about one hundred years ago. They were not generally
accepted until the end of the sixties when a law was passed officially
recognising them. The arrival of new cultural groups brought drastic
changes in the traditional ideas regarding funerals.

Hogebrug / Zuid-Holland

Suddenly trains are rushing past villages through green meadows,
past fields and woods, hurrying from one town to another.
From Utrecht to Woerden, then onto Gouda and beyond.
They never stop in Diemersbroek, Papekop or Hogebrug. Why trains
stop here and not there remains a mystery, or is it that the presence
of a station has to be justified commercially?

ABOVE: *Schalkwijk / Utrecht*   BELOW: *Schalkwijk / Utrecht*

ABOVE: *Hitsersekade / Zuid-Holland*

BELOW: *Nederslingeland / Zuid-Holland*

Railway bridges, motorways, viaducts and aqueducts
are indispensable for crossing canals, rivers, railways
and dikes. The Ministry of Public Works refers to
them as works of art. Not art in the literal sense
but art as a creative expression of mankind.

ABOVE: *Johan Werkmanpolder / Friesland* BELOW: *Lage Zwaluwe / Noord-Brabant*

ABOVE: *Beneden-Leeuwen / Gelderland*

The ingredients of concrete have been carefully thought out: sand, gravel and water. Cement is the glue that binds these ingredients together, and forms it into a hard, solid substance. Concrete is ideal for building. It is hard as stone and can withstand heavy loads.

BELOW: *Reiderwolderpolder / Groningen*

Its greatest advantage is that it can easily be moulded on the spot into any form or shape. Reputable architects have discovered the practical characteristics of concrete and often use it to implement their designs.

Eemland / Utrecht

Just to the north and east of the woodlands surrounding Blaricum and Baarn grasslands stretch for miles towards the distant horizon. This is the polder of Eemnes, the river basin of the Eem. At first sight rather monotonous until one glimpses the small creeks hidden amongst the reeds at the foot of the low dikes. A perfect environment for meadow birds. A few of these grasslands are owned and managed by The Society for the Preservation of Nature. This stretch of unspoilt polder gives the impression that enough land is available. But once the polder is inhabited and new farms appear this sense of space will sadly vanish.

Oost-Groningen

Towards the north the sturdy sea dike forms the border of
the vast lands of northeast Groningen. Parcels of land golden
with swaying wheat. Nowhere the fields are so immense as
here. Potato fields stretching as far as the eye can see.
It seems to be colder here in winter, and in the summer a
shimmer appears above the ground as in a desert.

Oost-Groningen

The European Union fixes the quotas for produce allotted to each country. As a result many farmers are forced to look for other sources of income. Their farms are turned into camping sites or stables for horses.

Nature societies seize the opportunity to buy farm-lands and turn them into nature reserves. The ratio between the two will be changing significantly in the coming years.

Flevopolder / Flevoland

Small planes fly over the extensive farmlands to spray insecticides on the crops. Tiny flags mark the area the pilot has to cover.

Scheemda / Groningen

Chalk and fertilizer are mostly used to improve the yield.
Profit and higher yield are gained at the expense of the
environment. More and more attention is being paid
to this development and the resulting damage.

Biesbosch / Noord-Brabant

All polders are enclosed by sturdy dikes to protect them.
One exception is the Land of Altena. The land to the west of
the A27 motorway gradually merges with Het Steurgat and the
Bakkers Kil, small streams running from the Hollandse Biesbosch,
a former tidal and flood area of creeks and channels. A case of
nature trying to survive alongside industrial sites.

Flevopolder / Flevoland

Avenues of trees, bushes, grass borders and flowers all
have their practical use. Their changing seasonal
colours are a direct contrast to the monotony
of man-made roads.

ABOVE: *Beutenaken / Limburg*

The debate on the importance of the environment is
ever increasing. Opinions on this differ greatly.
A tree is being felled, the moss is flowering, a seed is
growing, the last specimen disappears, a beetle dies,
a bird of prey is feeding its young with a field
mouse, the grass is gently swaying in the wind.

BELOWE: *Neerijnen / Gelderland*

In the distance the surveyors are approaching.
Then the disturbing noise of the bulldozers, or is it
the asphalt paving machine?

ABOVE: *Dreumel / Gelderland*

BELOW: *Dreumel / Gelderland*

With the fluctuating water levels in the water meadows along the Waal, trees and plants become completely or partially submerged. Each organism under water takes the opportunity to grow as fast as possible. This apparently pointless life dies when the water recedes.

ABOVE: *Dreumel / Gelderland*

Water, wind and willows. A flawless cliché.
A pollard-willow's cutting is planted in damp soil.
In spring the first cautious shoots are visible.
Twelve years later it has grown into a tree of such
proportions that it threatens to collapse under its
own weight.

BELOW: *Vijfheerenlanden / Zuid-Holland*

Farmers have no time left for the willows.
Groups of volunteers now pollard the trees so that
they can grow undisturbed for at least another
twelve years.

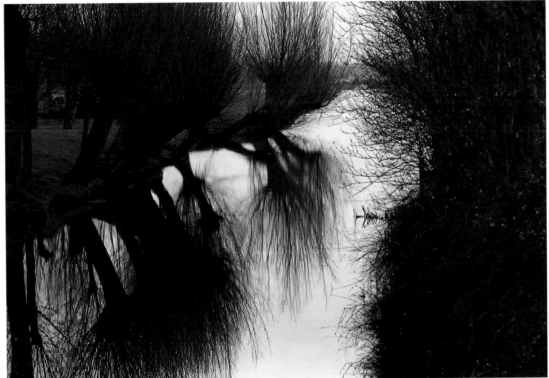

ABOVE: *Steenbergsevliet / Noord-Brabant*

Reeds are water plants belonging to the grass family, Gramineae. An easygoing plant which will grow almost anywhere.

BELOW: *Broek / Zuid-Holland*

Many men, plants and animals, whose livelihood or survival depend on reeds, derive their names from them: reed warblers, reed pheasants, reed wrens, reed-thatchers, reed-players, reed mace, reed canary grass. And even more plants and birds use the reeds as a safe haven.

Doornenburg / Gelderland

Land and water are often just grass and mud. It can also
mean poetry, a verse or a song. A sad song at times,
of water flooding the lands. At other times a joyous one.
The rains have finally arrived! It is all in the eye of the
beholder. On the one hand the pessimistic farmer,
on the other the lyrical poet.

Vuilendam / Zuid-Holland

Surveyors have found that the Alblasserwaard is sloping from east
to west. This has consequences for the land. From the higher
situated Gelderland the superfluous water streams down into the
polder in search of the lowest point near Kinderdijk.
A high dike to stem the water and technical expertise on drainage
and channelling protect the polder from floods.

Henschotermeer / Utrecht

The most attractive estates can be found in the hilly
wooded areas between Hilversum and Rhenen.
This area, together with the Veluwe, has less water than
elsewhere in the Netherlands. Here and there a small
lake with a sandy beach is used for recreation.

ABOVE: *Middelie / Noord-Holland*

BELOW: *Stellendam / Zuid-Holland*

The position of the sun and moon and the conditions on earth and water can jointly induce meteorological processes such as mist or wind or clouds floating past.

ABOVE: *Schenkeldijk / Zuid-Holland*

BELOW: *Schenkeldijk / Zuid-Holland*

A bend in the road, high bushes, an avenue of trees,
all might obscure the view when crossing.
This problem is easily solved by a strategically
placed traffic mirror.

Amsterdam Zuid-Oost / Noord-Holland

Architects are no longer required to build castles or imposing cathedrals. The few monarchs remaining already have their palaces and religious communities are not looking for large churches. The new "palaces" are now international trade centres, banks, museums and theatres.

World Trade Center / Amsterdam/Noord-Holland

In this age, where buildings as imposing as cathedrals, with huge glass façades, are springing up, the key-words seem to be world trade, communication, information technology, global.

ABOVE: *Maasvlakte / Zuid-Holland*

BELOW: *Europoort / Zuid-Holland*

Industrial production is, like so many other activities, changing constantly. Manufacturing means money and goods, but also problems such as waste and pollution in particular, sometimes even creating health hazards. Research is being carried out to find a solution to these problems.

ABOVE: *Europoort / Zuid-Holland*

BELOW: *Klundert / Noord-Brabant*

Waste, pollution and over production are global problems. Environmental issues are discussed internationally. Most countries are introducing far stricter legislation to ensure a healthier environment.

ABOVE: *IJmuiden / Hoogovens / Noord-Holland*   BELOW: *IJmuiden / Hoogovens / Noord-Holland*

A blast furnace is a melting furnace of some
50 meters in height. The steelworks, established in
1918 by bankers and the Dutch State, owes its
name, Hoogovens, to these imposing furnaces.

ABOVE: *Ridderkerk / Zuid-Holland*   BELOW: *Maasvlakte / Zuid-Holland*

Industry of all sorts creates jobs and contributes to
the welfare of the country. Fluctuations in supply
and demand influence the level of prosperity.

ABOVE: *Halsteren / Noord-Brabant*

BELOW: *Broek / Zuid-Holland*

The rows of countless slender poplars still fringe the horizon like fragile plumes. Poplars are a natural part of the Dutch landscape.

There is even a Society for Poplars and a National Poplar Committee, a feat which the oak and the dignified beech failed to achieve. They simply "belong" to the Society for the Protection of Trees.

ABOVE: *Zevenbergen / Noord-Brabant*

BELOW: *Zinkweg / Zuid-Holland*

All real estate, whether a house, factory, farm or tiny shed, is registered at the Land Registry offices. Changes must be reported here. A unique archive where buildings however small, and long gone, can be located to the last centimetre.

Arkel / Zuid-Holland

A narrow, tranquil road disappears into the mist.
It seems to dissolve into a void. The road as a modern
still-life. But that is not possible. A still-life is a painting
of inanimate objects. Or maybe it is possible.
After all the road is deadly quiet and the trees
are holding their breath.

Amsterdamse Bos / Amsterdam / Noord-Holland

The Amsterdamse Bos is more than sixty years old.
The woods, planted by unemployed in the early thirties,
are almost fully- grown and by now resemble a natural forest.
The many large greens, on which one can picnic or play foot-
ball, make this park attractive for recreation. Rowing is
possible on the Bosbaan and bicycles can be hired.

IJmuiden / Noord-Holland

The Noordzeekanaal enables ships to reach Amsterdam. A walk on the South pier, which projects into the sea for three kilometres at IJmuiden gives an exhilarating feeling of being in the middle of the sea. When the weather is fine and the sea is calm one can walk to the end of the pier, but during storms the pier is closed.

ABOVE: *Afsluitdijk / Friesland*

BELOW: *Nisse / Zeeland*

The Dutch are fond of their caravans. Their own
little home on wheels which they can take with them
anywhere. Nothing is more relaxing than stretching
out in front of one's own mini door.
Holland more than any other country has lost its
heart to the caravan.

ABOVE: *Hoek van Holland / Zuid-Holland*

BELOW: *Vlist / Zuid-Holland*

Everyone has this own ideas about how to
spend leisure time.

ABOVE: *Deventer / Overijssel*

Railway, road and river transport strongly compete for cargo and freight. Transport companies have their hands full with the transportation of "wet" and "dry" goods, or containers with bulky or general cargo.

BELOW: *Zaltbommel / Gelderland*

Freight is transported from Germany to Great Britain and vice versa through the Netherlands. Yet Deventer, Zwolle and northeast Groningen are also important destinations.

ABOVE: *Deventer / Overijssel*   BELOW: *Zwolle / Overijssel*

The construction of a bridge involves a large number of participants, each with their own specialist skills. Tenders and contracts have to be drawn up. Details of the structure need to be specified, the date of completion stated and the contract sum agreed upon.
The transportation and installation of prestressed

concrete beams, anchoring piers in the soft ground, setting up of electrically powered hydraulic displacement mechanisms, making of cantilevered side spans, plastering with resins, the vaulting, but also the finishing decorations to give the bridge an attractive appearance are all elements of bridge construction.

ABOVE: *Nieuwe Wetering / Zuid-Holland*   BELOW: *Ferwerd / Friesland*

ABOVE: *Hazerswoude-Dorp / Zuid-Holland*

Often older roads and paths tend to bend without obvious reason to the left or right. They have follo-wed their own course over the years, keeping their secrets to themselves. Maybe there used to be a farm, or maybe the path followed a stream, now no longer flowing.

BELOW: *Driebruggen / Zuid-Holland*

Nowadays roads are planned on drawing boards by civil engineers. Nothing is left to chance. For every obstacle there is a solution.

ABOVE: *Driebruggen / Zuid-Holland*　　　　　BELOW: *Everdingen / Diefdijk / Zuid-Holland*

Roads and paths are part of a larger network. This network differentiates between motorways, provincial roads, local roads, forest paths, streets, access roads, service roads, parallel roads, through-roads and dead-end roads, by-roads, railroads and waterways.

ABOVE: *Stormvloedkering / Zeeland*

BELOW: *Stormvloedkering / Zeeland*

Roads make their way over dikes, bridges, viaducts
and through tunnels and even under runways as at
Schiphol Airport. In Zeeland the road runs over the
prestigious Oosterschelde dam which protects the
land from the sea.

ABOVE: *Merwedekanaal / Utrecht*   BELOW: *Groot Ammers / Zuid-Holland*

Roads are the arteries along which man and traffic
are guided. The logistics of a country.

ABOVE: *Schenkeldijk / Zuid-Holland*

BELOW: *Flevopolder / Flevoland*

Roads consume traffic. Their purpose and location
determine to some extent the size of the road,
the lighting, the traffic signs and the road surface.
The latter ranges from cobblestones to asphalt.

Hobrede / Noord-Holland

The waterway of the Beemster and the Zeevang Polder
runs from Purmerend via the Beemsterringvaart to
Oosthuizen. Hobrede is more or less half way, on the
banks of the waterway: a small group of houses over-
looking a polder where cows are peacefully grazing.
The optimal cliché of the Netherlands as
a tourist attraction.

ABOVE: *Hei en Boeicop / Zuid-Holland*   BELOW: *Texel / Noord-Holland*

ABOVE: *Hindeloopen / Friesland*

Wouldn't it be marvellous if different colours were used for traffic signs. Canary yellow, cobalt blue or simply grey. Colours are chosen however for their effectiveness and not for their aesthetic value.

BELOW: *Zuid-Beijerland / Zuid-Holland*

Bright red and pure white are perhaps not the most elegant combination but certainly the most effective and therefore the safest.

Tempel / Zuid-Holland

There are more than three hundred thousand different species of plants. Pollution and climatic changes
cause many to disappear. On the other hand new
varieties appear through plant breeding and hybridi-
zation. They look very much like their wild species,
but have different characteristics.

Tempel / Zuid-Holland

ABOVE: *Honswijk / Utrecht*   BELOW: *Zurich / Friesland*

ABOVE: *Holwerd / Friesland*

BELOW: *Zurich/Friesland*

In the Netherlands everything is well-organised.
Everything has a place, a form, a purpose, to avoid
misunderstandings.
Then something unexpected turns up. A road sud-

denly disappears into a meadow, a strip of grass has
not been mown, or it doesn't turn white when
snow is falling.

ABOVE: *Dinteloord / Noord-Brabant*   BELOW: *Flevopolder / Flevoland*

ABOVE: *Achterhoek / Gelderland*

BELOW: *Delden / Overijssel*

To appreciate landscape one should look at it from different angles. A new perspective gives a whole new experience. Even classic painters tend to stick to the traditional setting of a scene. Photographers, however, have discovered the unlimited possibilities new perspectives have to offer.

ABOVE: *Veluwezoom / Gelderland*

Grass in a pasture is also nature. The farmer will look after it at regular intervals, fertilizing, mowing and making hay. A nature area supports an intricate system of natural elements.

BELOW: *Zuid-Beveland / Zeeland*

A complete ecological system where plants, birds, animals, insects, algae and fish are totally dependent on each other. Such nature areas can be found on untilled ground, the slopes of a dike, an abandoned meadow or woods surrounding a castle.

ABOVE: *Deest / Gelderland*   BELOW: *Uddel / Gelderland*

Special knowledge is required before one can discover
the ecological system of pools and lakes. Limnologists
are specialists studying the physical phenomena of lakes
and other fresh waters. This not only includes fish and
underwater plants but also microscopic unicellulars,
protozoa, such as flagellata.

ABOVE: *Buurserzand / Overijssel*   BELOW: *Veluwezoom / Gelderland*

ABOVE: *Kootwijkerzand / Gelderland*

BELOW: *Hoge Veluwe / Gelderland*

In the last century the marshy peat moors provided
valuable fuel, yet at the same time the excess water
became a problem. Defeating these problems has
given the Dutch indispensable know-how.
The sandy soils gave both problems and advantages -
sand drifts but also woods and timber.

Lemmer / Friesland

The lakes between Lemmer and Sneek are crowded in
the summer. Nearly every Dutchman has a strong
affinity with water, and many have their own boat.
Friesland was one of the most popular holiday destinations before travelling abroad became the fashion.

ABOVE: *Ursum / Noord-Holland*   BELOW: *Heeg / Friesland*

Wherever there is water, there is inevitably a sailing
school or a place to hire boats. Those who are lucky
enough to live alongside the water usually have their
own boat moored there. Drifting in a silent boat
towards evening, taking in the peace and quiet of the
surroundings, is the ideal setting for nature lovers.

ABOVE: *Neck / Noord-Holland*

BELOW: *Weipoort / Zuid-Holland*

Sitting on the banks of the water in the old peat
areas of North and South Holland, near the large
cities, one experiences an extraordinary feeling of
peace and quiet.

ABOVE: *Hindeloopen / Friesland*

BELOW: *Ketelmeer / Overijssel*

Sailing close to the wind, half wind or in front of the wind is the same for every sailing boat. Yet every boat has its own peculiarities. The sailing of a large vessel demands special skills if only because the captain has to shout the orders when the ship has to change course.

ABOVE: *Woudsend / Friesland*

BELOW: *Hellevoetsluis / Zuid-Holland*

Tacking is a technique which is used when sailing
into the wind. Making use of the physics of wind
and water to sail. Once one is adept a race might
be attempted.

ABOVE: *Numansdorp / Zuid-Holland*   BELOW: *Katwijk / Zuid-Holland*

ABOVE: *Katwijk / Zuid-Holland*

BELOW: *Cartierheide / Noord-Brabant*

Each generation has its own pace and interests. Days are spent with friends and colleagues of the same age. Usually it is only at weddings and funerals that the generations mix.

ABOVE: *Arkel / Zuid-Holland*

Dutch paper currency is colourful and has beautiful illustrations depicting a lighthouse, a bird, a sunflower. Strangely enough windmills have been omitted on banknotes.

BELOW: *Lopik / Utrecht*

The windmill should have deserved this place of honour as it was the windmill that created the country we are now inhabiting. Without them the Netherlands would merely have been a narrow strip of land.

ABOVE: *Loenen aan de Vecht / Utrecht*　　　　　BELOW: *Broek in Waterland / Noord-Holland*

Despite family planning the population is still on the
increase. More and more people are looking for
adequate housing. The government submits a plan
to build more than 50,000 homes over the next few
years. The magnitude of a town.

ABOVE: *Hindeloopen / Friesland*

BELOW: *Austerlitz / Utrecht*

Sport, entertainment and enjoying nature is
more than simply distraction. It also satisfies a
psychological need.

Zeddam / Gelderland

A carriage is a four-wheeled vehicle drawn by one or
more horses. At the beginning of this century it was
quite usual to travel this way. Nowadays many taxi
companies own a number of these carriages which they
hire out for weddings.

Pier / IJmuiden / Noord-Holland

ISBN 90-6255-636-1

MDCCCCLXXXXV
© Martin Kers and Terra Publishing, Warnsveld

Colophon

Photo's: Martin Kers
Photo on page 5: Oerlemans van Reeken Studio: Joop van Reeken
Text: Marijke Kers
Translation: Margriet J. Maurenbrecher
Design: Teo van Gerwen Design, Leende
Lithography and print: Tesink, Zutphen
Binding: Callenbach, Nijkerk